A Cricket Came to Church

Design and Production by Daniela K. Robins
Robins Wings Publishing Company
Chesapeake, Virginia

Ruby E. Weeks

I would first like to give thanks to my Lord and Savior, Jesus Christ. He saved my soul and gave me the heart to serve Him. He has also taken me through many a "training process" before I was prepared to answer His call. I also would like to thank Daniela Robins for her talents and abilities to make this publication possible.

A cricket came to church
one day.

Folks were just a few in number,

but oh, what they had to say.

The songs they sang were
not of today,

songs of old, but still songs
of praise!

"The Old Account Was Settled Long Ago,"

"I Must Tell Jesus,"

"Nearer My God To Thee,"

and "Rock Of Ages Cleft For Me."

The songs fired up the preacher,
and he began to preach.

The cricket also tried to speak, but all he could do was chirp.

This caused a great commotion; oh my,
what a stir!

They picked him up gently and quickly put him outside. (This the cricket did not like).

The preacher's message needed
to be heard.

But that cricket wanted to chirp.

He did not understand that he was being rude because he would not be quiet in this part of the service as he should.

The preacher got back to preaching,

but from somewhere outside,
that cricket kept on singing

since he wasn't allowed to
worship in the church.

Moral of this story: when you're
not accepted in one place,

don't give up and quit.

Keep seeking God's will until you finish life's race.

You will not please everyone.

And even those who love the Lord may be on a different timing than you'd like.

Keep seeking the Lord and
obeying what He says.

Don't get discouraged and quit.

Do God's will for your life. He has a plan, a place, and a purpose for you.

His love is faithful and true.

But He has a time for you to begin what He calls you to do.

Just keep trusting Him, and the Lord
will see you through.

" (For he saith, I have heard thee in a time accepted, And in the day of salvation have I succoured thee: behold, now is the accepted time; behold, now is the day of salvation.)"

2 Corinthians 6:2 KJV

www.ingramcontent.com/pod-product-compliance
Lightning Source LLC
Chambersburg PA
CBHW042126040426
42450CB00002B/80